The story of
ROBOTS

Leonbattista Donati

Illustrated by
Lorenzo Cecchi, Francesca d'Ottavi, Claudia Saraceni,
Daniela Sarcina, Ivan Stalio

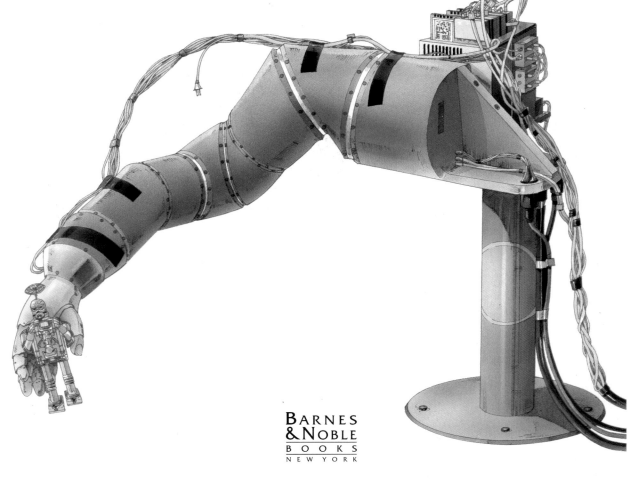

BARNES
&NOBLE
BOOKS
NEW YORK

DoGi

Produced by
Donati Giudici
Associati, Florence
Original title:
La storia dei robot
Text:
Leonbattista Donati
Illustrations:
Boni-Galante Studio
(Simone Boni, Lorenzo
Cecchi, Ivan Stalio),
Francesca d'Ottavi,
Carlo Ferrantini, Gianni
Mazzoleni, Claudia
Saraceni, Daniela
Sarcina, Sergio,
Donato Spedaliere
Design:
Giuseppe Arrighi,
Laura Davis
English translation:
Simon Knight
Editor, English edition:
Ruth Nason
Typesetting:
Ken Alston,
A.J. Latham Ltd

© 1995 Donati
Giudici Associati s.r.l.
Florence, Italy
First English-
language edition
© 1996 Watts Books

First American edition
© 1997
Barnes & Noble, Inc.
This edition published by
Barnes & Noble, Inc. by
arrangement with DoGi srl

ISBN
0-7607-0595-X

HOW TO USE THIS BOOK

THE MAIN TEXT
On each double
page, the text under
the main title gives
an overview of the
topic covered.

ILLUSTRATIONS
One or more large
illustrations show
tools and machines
and how they were
used. These range
from the simplest
hand tools to
sophisticated
robots.

**FURTHER
INFORMATION**
Smaller drawings
and photographs
introduce scientific
principles,
examples and
important people
connected with the
topic under study.

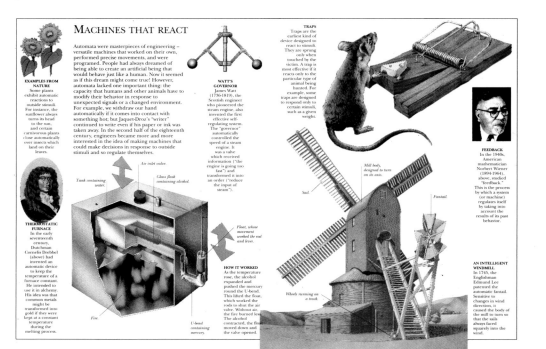

MACHINES THAT REACT

Automata were masterpieces of engineering – versatile machines that worked on their own, performed precise movements, and were programed. People had always dreamed of being able to create an artificial being that would behave just like a human. Now it seemed as if this dream might come true! However, automata lacked one important thing: the capacity that humans and other animals have to modify their behavior in response to unexpected signals or a changed environment. For example, we withdraw our hand automatically if it comes into contact with something hot; but Jaquet-Droz's "writer" continued to write even if his paper or ink was taken away. In the second half of the eighteenth century, engineers became more and more interested in the idea of making machines that could make decisions in response to outside stimuli and so regulate themselves.

EXAMPLES FROM NATURE
Some plants exhibit automatic reactions to outside stimuli. For instance, the sunflower always turns its head to the sun, and certain carnivorous plants close automatically over insects which land on their leaves.

THERMOSTATIC FURNACE
In the early seventeenth century, Dutchman Cornelis Drebbel (above) had invented an automatic device to keep the temperature of a furnace constant. He intended to use it in alchemy. His idea was that common metals might be transformed into gold if they were kept at a constant temperature during the melting process.

Air inlet valve.

Tank containing water.

Glass flask containing alcohol.

WATT'S GOVERNOR
James Watt (1736-1819), the Scottish engineer who pioneered the steam engine, also invented the first effective self-regulating system. The "governor" automatically controlled the speed of a steam engine. It was a valve which received information ("the engine is going too fast") and transformed it into an order ("reduce the input of steam").

Float, whose movement worked the rod and lever.

HOW IT WORKED
As the temperature rose, the alcohol expanded and pushed the mercury round the U-bend. This lifted the float, which worked the rods to shut the air valve. Without air, the fire burned less. The alcohol contracted, the float moved down and the valve opened.

Fire.

U-bend containing mercury.

TRAPS
Traps are the earliest kind of device designed to react to stimuli. They are sprung only when touched by the victim. A trap is most effective if it reacts only to the particular type of animal being hunted. For example, some traps are designed to respond only to certain stimuli, such as a given weight.

Mill body, designed to turn on its axis.

Sail.

Fantail.

FEEDBACK
In the 1940s, American mathematician Norbert Wiener (1894-1964), above, studied "feedback." This is the process by which a system (or machine) regulates itself by taking into account the results of its past behavior.

AN INTELLIGENT WINDMILL
In 1745, the Englishman Edmund Lee patented the automatic fantail. Sensitive to changes in wind direction, it caused the body of the mill to turn so that the sails always faced squarely into the wind.

Wheels running on a track.

HISTORICAL BACKGROUND
Each topic is set in a historical context, to show the reasons for and consequences of new developments.

IMPORTANT PEOPLE
Information is provided about people who have contributed to research and development.

Particular thanks are expressed to Professor Jean-Pierre Merlet, Director of Research at INRIA, Sophia-Antipolis, France, for his advice; and to Professor Shigeki Sugano, Department of Mechanical Engineering, Waseda University, Tokyo, for the loan of photographs.

For picture credits, see page 47.

CONTENTS

THE STORY OF TECHNOLOGY

DAEDALUS

Greek mythology also tells of Daedalus, who builds a labyrinth for King Minos of Crete. He falls from favor and is imprisoned by the king, but escapes with his son Icarus by making wings and flying away.
  In this story, technology is no longer a gift of the gods but the fruit of human intelligence.

The history of technology dates back three million years, to the first primitive stone tools. It is divided into three stages. The first was by far the longest, as human beings looked for ways of extending what they could do with their hands. They invented tools, the lever, and increasingly complex machines, which had the effect of magnifying their own dexterity and strength. The second stage saw the invention of machines which replaced human labor. A typical development was the mill, where machinery was no longer worked by human strength but by forms of energy such as water and wind. During the third stage, humans have been almost entirely freed from hard physical work and so can concentrate on commanding and controlling the machines they have invented. We are living in this third stage, which itself breaks down into two periods. The age of mechanical engineering began with the first clocks and culminated in the programable machines of the eighteenth century. Then came the age of electricity and electronics, leading to the creation of robots: machines controlled by humans to take their place in performing complex, difficult and dangerous tasks.

GAINING CONTROL

The first tools were invented in the Paleolithic period (the Old Stone Age). With these tools, humans achieved greater control over the world around them. It became possible to perform tasks, such as cutting and digging, that could not be done with the hands alone, and also to handle very hot objects and so work with fire.

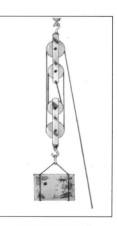

INCREASING STRENGTH

The ancient Greeks made a distinction between simple machines – the lever, the inclined plane, the screw, the pulley, the wedge and the winch – and complex machines combining the action of two or more simple devices. The strength of humans on their own is limited. The effect of early machines was to magnify human strength.

CRANES

The ancient Romans built cranes. These were complex machines, combining the principle of the winch and the use of pulleys.

WORKING ON ITS OWN
Applying wind or water power to a machine creates a mechanical device which can run on its own. An example is a mill grinding corn. In this case, all the miller has to do is check and regulate the speed of the machinery.

ELECTRICITY AND ELECTRONICS
Electricity has revolutionized the way in which machines are controlled, while electronics has given them extraordinary powers of memory.

CLOCKWORK
A clock or watch is a device which performs a simple task without human assistance: moving its hands at equal, regular intervals.

ROBOTS
The most widespread use of robots is in industry. These robots are usually one-armed machines programed to perform complex tasks. They can carry out these tasks repeatedly and quickly, without getting tired as human workers would do. The robots used in other fields, such as surgery and space exploration, also tend to be single-armed machines. However, they normally work very slowly, because the delicate tasks they are programed to perform need to be done with great care.

MEMORY
A musical box is a mechanical instrument programed to play a tune. The memory of this one is a cylinder with teeth.

AUTOMATA
Automata are devices which imitate the actions of living creatures. Eighteenth-century ones, programed to perform highly complex actions, reached a peak of mechanical ingenuity and precision. Some, with the gestures of human musicians, could play several tunes. It was a maker of automata, Jacques de Vaucanson, who first applied the principles of their construction to industrial machines.

SCIENCE FICTION
The robots described in science fiction appear vaguely human. They move around, are almost as independent as human beings, have extraordinary intelligence and are aware of their environment. They are purely imaginary. It is unlikely that any such robots will be designed and built in the near future.

ARMS AND HANDS

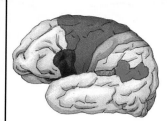

All animals are equipped to act on the world around them. They have the means to obtain food, build nests or dens, attack other animals, defend themselves or hide away. Birds have beaks, cats claws, elephants trunks. Humans are especially well equipped. The combination of hand and arm is one of the most elaborate mechanisms found in nature. The arm gives strength and movement, while the function of the hand is to hold objects. The hand is an extremely sensitive and flexible instrument, able to vary its grip according to the type, weight and size of the object concerned.

SENDING INSTRUCTIONS
The brain sends messages to the hand and arm muscles, which control grip and movement. Information about the tightness of the grip and the position of the limb travels to the brain from nerve endings in the hand and arm. The part of the brain which controls hands and arms is far more developed than the part responsible for the movement of the legs.

CLAWS, BEAKS AND TONGUES
While humans have hands, other animals use claws, beaks or prehensile tongues to hunt prey, obtain food or defend themselves against predators.

Fingertips have large numbers of nerve endings. These are sensitive to the slightest touch and to temperature and pain.

The elbow is a spherical joint, enabling the forearm to move in two ways: it can bend and rotate.

The wrist allows the hand to move independently of the arm. Its main purpose is to position the hand for different tasks.

KEEPING A FIRM GRIP

The hand has its limitations when it comes to holding wet or slippery objects. To hold such objects more securely, some robots are fitted with an attachment like an elephant's trunk.

THE ELEPHANT'S TRUNK

About five feet (1.5 m) long, the elephant's trunk is formed from the animal's nose and upper lip. It can pick up an egg without breaking it and lift objects weighing as much as six hundred pounds (272 kg). The elephant's trunk rivals the human arm for efficiency.

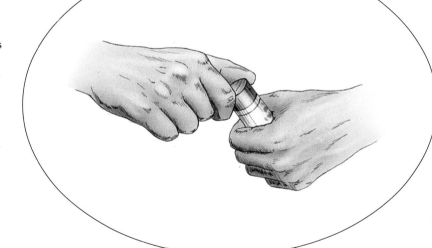

TWO HANDS AT WORK

Working together, the hands can perform more complex tasks. They tend to specialize: for example, if you are right-handed, the left hand ensures a tight grip and the right hand does the precision work.

DIFFERENT GRIPS

Each finger of the hand has three joints and is independent of the others. The thumb acts in opposition to the fingers. This arrangement makes it possible for the hand to grip in many different ways.

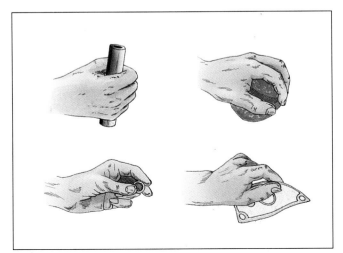

ROBOT HAND

If a machine is to carry out human tasks, it is best to fit it with an attachment similar to a human hand.

FROM HANDS TO HAND TOOLS

The hand-arm system is a highly developed natural instrument, but there are limits to its strength, toughness, reach and accuracy. For example, the hand is not designed for cutting or piercing tasks. It cannot touch fire or sharp or pointed objects without risk of injury. Although it can do fine, detailed work, it is unable to manipulate very small objects. To overcome these limitations, humans through history have gradually developed many different kinds of specialized tools: some for cutting, some for boring, and others, for instance, for operating in hostile environments. By making and using tools, people have vastly increased their ability to influence the world around them.

HANDS
With their many blood vessels and nerve endings, hands are sensitive and also delicate. Doing lots of manual work makes the skin tougher, but also tends to make it less sensitive.

ANIMALS USING TOOLS
Humans are not the only creatures to use tools. The woodpecker finch and the mangrove finch, for instance, use cactus spines to extract insects from tree trunks. However, humans are the only creatures to design and make tools.

GLOVES
A glove protects the hand, enabling it to operate in hostile environments which a bare hand could not cope with. A glove is therefore a kind of tool, acting as an intermediary between hand and environment.

REACH
It is difficult to scrub your own back without the help of a brush. This is a simple example of extending the reach of the hand-arm system.

CUTTING TOOLS

Looking at the history of cutting tools, from the earliest stone chippings (known as flakes) to modern steel knives, we can see how people have always tried to develop more effective and specialized instruments.

REACHING FURTHER

For picking up objects which are out of normal reach, there are tools which mimic the hand-arm system. Here, for example, the pole is like an extended arm and the pincers like a hand.

TOUCHING FIRE

A blacksmith uses pincers for taking red-hot metal from the forge. Pokers and tongs, used for tending open fires, are other tools which enable us to touch fire.

STRIKING

The hand-arm system on its own cannot drive a nail into wood. The tool needed for this task is a hammer. The handle acts as a lever: the longer the handle, the greater the force exerted on the nail head.

HANDLING SMALL OBJECTS

The smaller the objects you try to manipulate with your fingers, the more difficult it becomes to work precisely. To assemble the tiny components of a clock or watch, clockmakers use tweezers and extremely small screwdrivers.

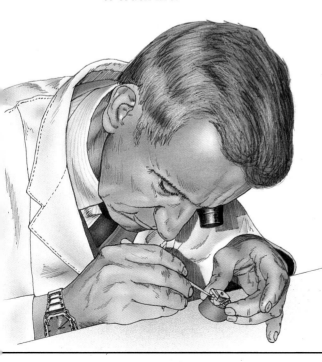

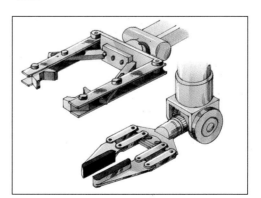

SPECIALIZED ROBOT HANDS

Industrial robots have several interchangeable hands for specialized purposes, one for each task they are required to perform.

POWERFUL MACHINES

Human muscular strength is limited; it is certainly inferior to the power of many species of animal. At a very early stage in their development, human beings must have realized that their ability to act on the world around them, and indeed their very survival, depended on finding ways to increase their rather small physical strength. They achieved this by making and developing tools. A particularly important discovery was that a simple stick could be transformed into a lever. This was the first step on the road to inventing machines capable of multiplying a small input of human energy by ten or even a hundred times. The ancient Romans used cranes when they built their great monuments. These machines were like enormously powerful arms, capable of lifting huge stones and moving them into position. The crane was the most ingenious and powerful complex machine invented in ancient times. Nevertheless, a great deal of human effort was still needed to work and control it.

THE FOREARM
Chess players typically sit with an elbow resting on the table. With the arm in this position, it is possible to move the hand with great accuracy, even if you are manipulating objects much heavier than chess pieces. The force exerted by the arm is minimal, because the muscles are used only to balance the weight. This is the principle on which many early cranes worked.

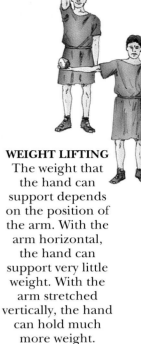

WEIGHT LIFTING
The weight that the hand can support depends on the position of the arm. With the arm horizontal, the hand can support very little weight. With the arm stretched vertically, the hand can hold much more weight.

The jib or arm, of the crane was moved to left or right by tightening the ropes on one side and slacking-off on the ropes on the opposite side.

This rope was for raising and lowering the jib.

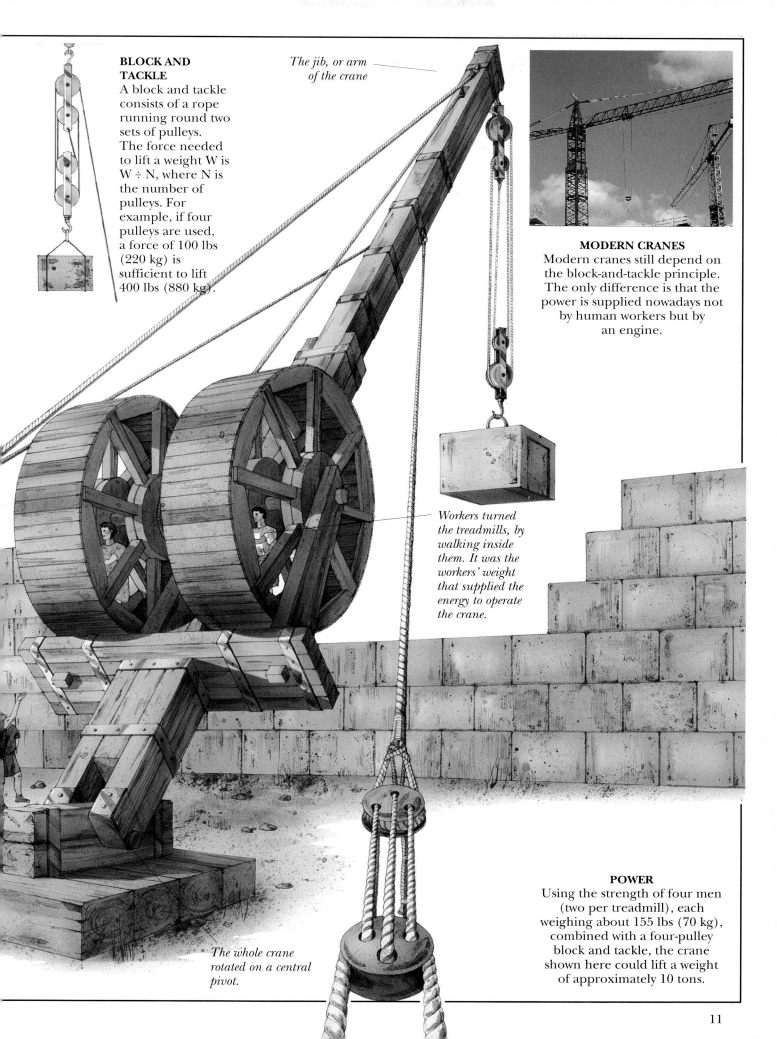

BLOCK AND TACKLE

A block and tackle consists of a rope running round two sets of pulleys. The force needed to lift a weight W is W ÷ N, where N is the number of pulleys. For example, if four pulleys are used, a force of 100 lbs (220 kg) is sufficient to lift 400 lbs (880 kg).

The jib, or arm of the crane

MODERN CRANES

Modern cranes still depend on the block-and-tackle principle. The only difference is that the power is supplied nowadays not by human workers but by an engine.

Workers turned the treadmills, by walking inside them. It was the workers' weight that supplied the energy to operate the crane.

The whole crane rotated on a central pivot.

POWER

Using the strength of four men (two per treadmill), each weighing about 155 lbs (70 kg), combined with a four-pulley block and tackle, the crane shown here could lift a weight of approximately 10 tons.

TAKING CONTROL

By domesticating the ox and training it to pull a plow, humans achieved three things: they increased their productivity, saved themselves a lot of physical effort, and gained time and energy to concentrate on the quality of their work, plowing straight furrows and breaking the soil to the correct depth. It was a revolutionary change, from plowing the land themselves to guiding and controlling animals to do the work for them. Later, a similar revolutionary change took place in the way people powered their machines: instead of working the machines by hand, themselves, they learned to harness forms of energy, such as water, wind and steam, to do the work for them. By inventing machines which, to some extent, worked on their own (sometimes called "autonomous" machines), people became free to direct, regulate and control.

TRAINED ANIMALS

A well-trained horse understands instructions from its rider and stops or turns when ordered to do so. The rider controls the horse by speaking to it or pulling on the reins: a code to which the animal has learned to respond.

AT THE WHEEL

By turning the steering wheel, a driver changes the alignment of the front wheels of his or her car. As the wheels are powered by the engine, the car itself turns in the desired direction. The driver simply transmits orders via the steering wheel.

AT THE HELM

A sailing boat is driven by the wind, but the sailor steers the craft in the direction wanted, by adjusting the rudder and sails. Compared with the power of the wind, the energy needed to move the tiller, to turn the rudder, is minimal.

THE PLOW
In traditional agriculture, oxen provide the power. The farmer's job is to make sure that the plowshare runs through the soil at the right depth and that the animal stays on course, so that straight, even furrows are plowed.

THE WATER MILL
Water is channeled away to fall on to the blades of this mill wheel and make it turn. The rotation of the wheel is passed on, via shafts, to the millstones. By regulating the flow of water, the miller ensures a constant energy supply.

THE VERSATILITY OF A MILL

First, people invented tools which extended their control over the world around them. Then came powerful machines, and later machines that worked on their own. People also realized the need for a machine to be versatile, able to perform a number of different tasks. Mills, powered by wind or water, were the first machines to have this advantage. Originally they were used to grind corn or other substances, but gradually ingenious devices were introduced to enable them to perform other functions: working hammers, mallets, saws and bellows. From classical times until the invention of the steam engine in the eighteenth century, the mill was the only machine to combine power, the ability to work on its own and versatility.

A HAND MILL
A back-and-forth movement of the arm causes the hand mill to turn. The same principle also works in reverse: the turning of a water-wheel can be converted into back-and-forward movement.

MILLSTONES
Grain placed between the two millstones is ground into flour. If the mill wheel turns too quickly, it causes the flour to be scorched.

Lantern-pinion.

FRICTION
A moving part of a machine may rub against another part. This rubbing, or friction, slows down the movement. Heat is generated where the two parts rub, and they can become worn. Greasing or oiling the machine parts helps reduce friction.

Friction is reduced by cylindrical bearings, which serve to cut down the area of contact between fixed and moving parts. Wooden bearings were first used in the fifteenth century.

The rotation of the horizontal shaft is passed along to the vertical shaft by a cogwheel. The teeth, or cogs, of the turning wheel push the upright bars of the lantern-pinion, turning the shaft it surrounds.

Reversing the belt reverses the direction of movement imparted to the shaft.

ELECTRICITY
With the advent of electricity at the end of the nineteenth century, mechanical transmission was no longer so important. Electrical impulses could now be used to control machines from a distance.

Drive belts or chains are used to transmit motion from an energy source to a machine some distance away.

A crank is an elbow-like part on a rotating shaft. Used in conjunction with a connecting rod, it converts circular to back-and-forward motion. This device was first used in the late fifteenth century.

Cam.

A crank and connecting rod are used to work a pump.

Projections on a rotating shaft, known as cams, are here used to trip a hammer. The cams convert the continuous movement of the shaft into alternating movement of the hammer.

Here the rotation of the shaft has been converted into back-and-forward motion, to work a saw.

As regular as clockwork

As sources of energy, wind and water are never entirely predictable and cannot be expected to turn a windmill's sails or a watermill's wheel at a constant speed. Millers have come up with various methods for controlling the speed of their machinery, but the results have never been exact. In fact, as long as the main requirement is for a machine to be powerful, complete regularity of motion is not important. By contrast, if you are making clocks – devices designed to mark and measure time – it is essential to find a way of converting a natural, irregular source of energy into precise, regular movement. Clock-makers therefore invented ever more refined and accurate mechanisms. They developed systems for regulating motion, such as the foliot (weighted cross-bar) and, later, the pendulum.

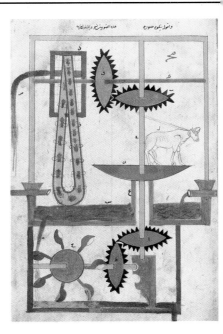

AL-JAZARI
In Mesopotamia in 1206, Al-Jazari published a treatise on mechanics, illustrating a variety of water clocks and hydraulic machines. One of the latter is shown above.

WHEN THE COCK CROWS
The clock of Strasbourg cathedral, built in 1352, featured a rooster which would emerge every hour, lift its head, flap its wings and crow three times.

The overflow pipe ensures that the funnel is always full, so that water flows into the container below at a constant rate.

WATER CLOCKS
Ancient Greek inventors were the first to build simple water clocks. The picture here shows a sixteenth-century reconstruction of an ancient Greek idea. Water flowed into a container and, as the level rose, lifted a float which was connected by a gearing mechanism to hands mounted on a clock face. The problem was to ensure that the water in the container rose steadily, so that the hands moved at a constant speed.

MECHANICAL FIGURES
Many medieval clocks featured mechanical figures designed to perform simple lifelike movements. For example, the Moors of St. Mark's clock in Venice strike the bell with a hammer every hour.

The foliot was a horizontal cross-bar, connected to a spindle called the verge. The verge and foliot turned first one way, then the other.

The speed at which the foliot turned could be adjusted by altering the positions of two small weights.

THE WEIGHT
The first mechanical clocks were driven by a falling weight attached to a cord wound around a drum. The problem was that the weight tended to drop faster as the cord unwound. Regulating the movement called for great skill on the part of clockmakers.

MECHANICAL CLOCKS
Mechanical clocks first appeared in Europe in the thirteenth century. The main components were a weight, to supply the energy; an escapement, to transfer energy from the power source to the counting mechanism; the hands; and the foliot, which regulated the movement.

The rotation of the large toothed wheel was passed, via pinions and further wheels, to the verge. The pins on the escape wheel (top) made the verge turn in alternating directions.

A COILED SPRING
When compressed, a coiled spring is a store of potential energy. Releasing the spring transforms that energy into kinetic (moving) energy. The transformation may be very fast, as in the flipper of a pinball machine; or slow and even, as in a watch, where the spring is regulated by a balance wheel.

THE METRONOME
Galileo (1564-1642) showed that the frequency at which a pendulum swings depends on its length. This is the principle behind a metronome. A weight is moved up or down along a rigid pendulum. The greater the distance between the weight and the bottom of the pendulum, the faster the metronome beats.

FROM CLOCKS TO AUTOMATA

By the eighteenth century, clockmakers had developed and refined the workings of mechanical clocks so much, that some of the them chose to concentrate instead on building automata. These were lifelike mechanical figures, worked by clockwork, which imitated human or animal movement. They were a source of great wonder for the eighteenth-century public. Their makers were not simply producing expensive toys, although that is how it may seem. They were experimenting with philosophies of the time: in particular, with the idea that living organisms could be understood as extraordinary machines. The result was a big step forward in the way people thought about machines. Automata showed that machines could be designed to perform not just one repetitive movement, but a large number of different movements in a pre-arranged sequence. To do this, a machine needed a complex mechanism and a "memory" in which to store instructions. The idea of the programable machine was born, and some scientists have no hesitation in describing automata as the ancestors of modern robots.

THE DROZ FAMILY
Pierre Jaquet-Droz (1721-1790) and his son Henri-Louis (1752-1791), from Switzerland, became famous throughout Europe as makers of automata. Three of their child androids were Charles, who could write several sentences with his quill pen; Marianne, who played the harpsichord; and Henry, the artist. Above: Henri-Louis Jaquet-Droz.

HENRY DROZ
This automaton was programed to draw four different pictures, and would blow on the paper at regular intervals to clear it of dust.

THE DRUMMER GIRL
This automaton was made in 1785 by the German craftsman Kining. It was bought by Queen Marie-Antoinette of France. The photograph shows the toothed cylinder and cams which controlled the movements of the figure.

INSIDE
Henry was worked by a set of cams mounted on a cylinder turned by clockwork. He had a bellows mechanism in his head. It took years to create a perfect automaton.

MUSICAL BOX
The sound of a musical box is made by the teeth on the cylinder plucking thin metal blades of varying lengths. The cylinder is the box's "memory." A tune is transcribed on to it in the form of a code: each note is represented by one or more teeth, positioned so that they pluck the appropriate metal blade or blades.

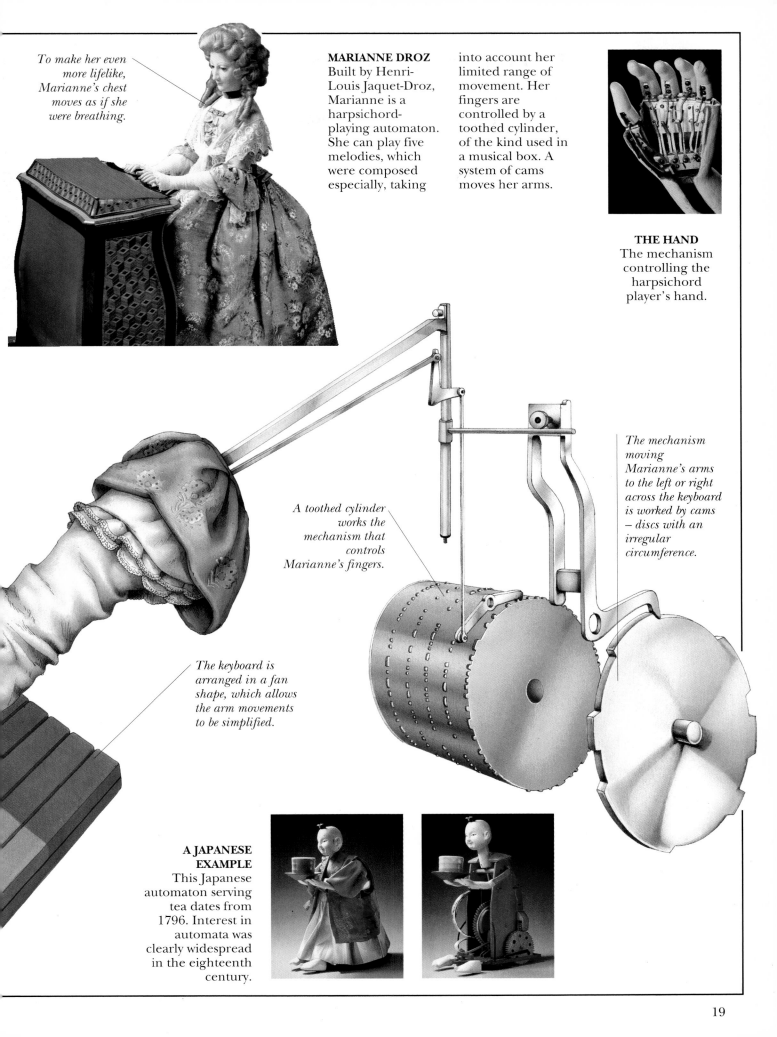

To make her even more lifelike, Marianne's chest moves as if she were breathing.

MARIANNE DROZ
Built by Henri-Louis Jaquet-Droz, Marianne is a harpsichord-playing automaton. She can play five melodies, which were composed especially, taking into account her limited range of movement. Her fingers are controlled by a toothed cylinder, of the kind used in a musical box. A system of cams moves her arms.

THE HAND
The mechanism controlling the harpsichord player's hand.

A toothed cylinder works the mechanism that controls Marianne's fingers.

The mechanism moving Marianne's arms to the left or right across the keyboard is worked by cams – discs with an irregular circumference.

The keyboard is arranged in a fan shape, which allows the arm movements to be simplified.

A JAPANESE EXAMPLE
This Japanese automaton serving tea dates from 1796. Interest in automata was clearly widespread in the eighteenth century.

MACHINES THAT REACT

Automata were masterpieces of engineering – versatile machines that worked on their own, performed precise movements, and were programed. People had always dreamed of being able to create an artificial being that would behave just like a human. Now it seemed as if this dream might come true! However, automata lacked one important thing: the capacity that humans and other animals have to modify their behavior in response to unexpected signals or a changed environment. For example, we withdraw our hand automatically if it comes into contact with something hot; but Jaquet-Droz's "writer" continued to write even if his paper or ink was taken away. In the second half of the eighteenth century, engineers became more and more interested in the idea of making machines that could make decisions in response to outside stimuli and so regulate themselves.

EXAMPLES FROM NATURE
Some plants exhibit automatic reactions to outside stimuli. For instance, the sunflower always turns its head to the sun, and certain carnivorous plants close automatically over insects which land on their leaves.

THERMOSTATIC FURNACE
In the early seventeenth century, Dutchman Cornelis Drebbel (above) had invented an automatic device to keep the temperature of a furnace constant. He intended to use it in alchemy. His idea was that common metals might be transformed into gold if they were kept at a constant temperature during the melting process.

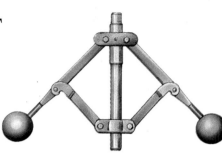

WATT'S GOVERNOR
James Watt (1736-1819), the Scottish engineer who pioneered the steam engine, also invented the first effective self-regulating system. The "governor" automatically controlled the speed of a steam engine. It was a valve which received information ("the engine is going too fast") and transformed it into an order ("reduce the input of steam").

Air inlet valve.

Glass flask containing alcohol.

Tank containing water.

Float, whose movement worked the rod and lever.

Fire.

HOW IT WORKED
As the temperature rose, the alcohol expanded and pushed the mercury round the U-bend. This lifted the float, which worked the rods to shut the air valve. Without air, the fire burned less. The alcohol contracted, the float moved down and the valve opened.

U-bend containing mercury.

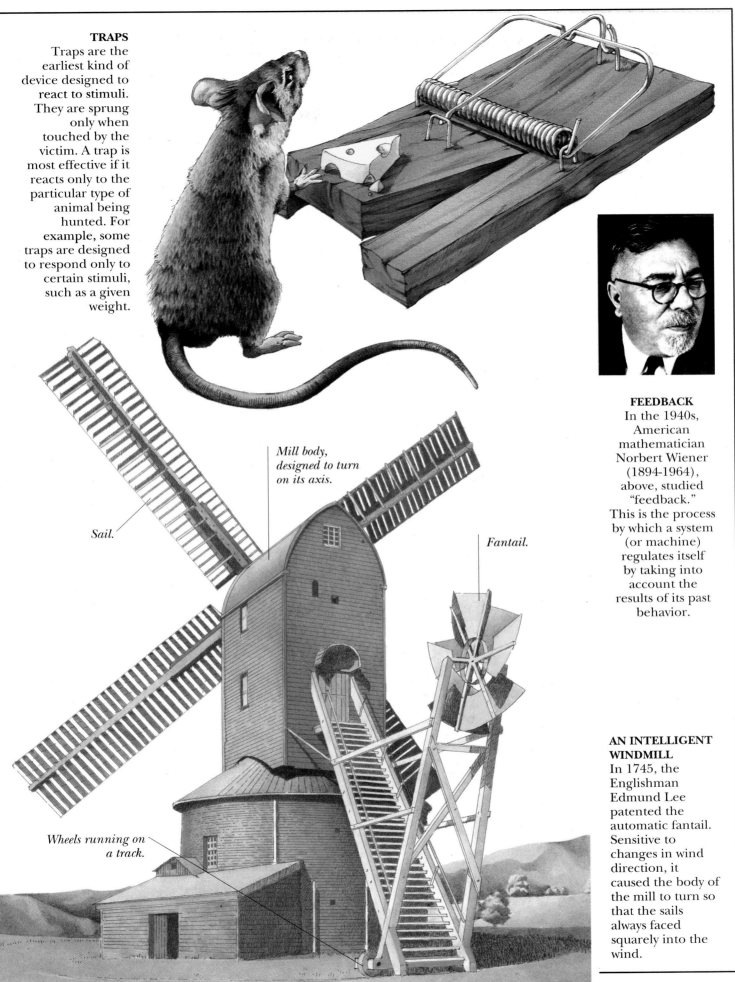

TRAPS
Traps are the earliest kind of device designed to react to stimuli. They are sprung only when touched by the victim. A trap is most effective if it reacts only to the particular type of animal being hunted. For example, some traps are designed to respond only to certain stimuli, such as a given weight.

Sail.

Mill body, designed to turn on its axis.

Fantail.

Wheels running on a track.

FEEDBACK
In the 1940s, American mathematician Norbert Wiener (1894-1964), above, studied "feedback." This is the process by which a system (or machine) regulates itself by taking into account the results of its past behavior.

AN INTELLIGENT WINDMILL
In 1745, the Englishman Edmund Lee patented the automatic fantail. Sensitive to changes in wind direction, it caused the body of the mill to turn so that the sails always faced squarely into the wind.

PUNCHED CARDS

JACQUES DE VAUCANSON
(1709-1782)
At eighteen, de Vaucanson broke religious vows to pursue a career as an inventor. He became famous for his automata, including a figure that played eleven tunes on the flute. Abandoning the project of creating an artificial human being, he accepted the job of restructuring the silk industry, a task in which he revealed great talent as an organizer.

In 1741, the King of France wanted to appoint someone to organize the restructuring of the French silk industry. He chose Jacques de Vaucanson, a celebrated constructor of automata. In a short time, drawing on his wide experience of machinery, de Vaucanson simplified weaving looms and introduced programing systems. To increase efficiency, he divided the weavers' work into precise, repetitive tasks, as if they were to be performed by the different components of an automaton. Sixty years later, Joseph Marie Jacquard completed de Vaucanson's work. He added an ingenious but simple attachment to the loom, which enabled a weaver to produce materials with a complex pattern as easily as single-color fabrics. This device was based on a system of punched cards, which controlled the way the machine worked. The method was already known, but Jacquard brought it to perfection. In 1833, an Englishman, Charles Babbage, adopted the idea of punched cards when he designed an "analytical machine," the forerunner of modern computers.

REACTIONS
Industrialists greatly appreciated the Jacquard loom. They soon introduced over 10,000 of them in their factories. On the other hand, the weavers saw the loom as a threat to their livelihoods. In 1812, in Lyon, they destroyed one of the machines, to dramatize their fear.

JOSEPH MARIE JACQUARD
(1752-1834)
Jacquard was the son of a poor weaver. It was in 1790 that he conceived the idea for the loom which is named after him. But, because he lacked capital, he had to wait ten years before he could complete his invention. The Jacquard loom was presented at the Paris Exhibition of 1801.

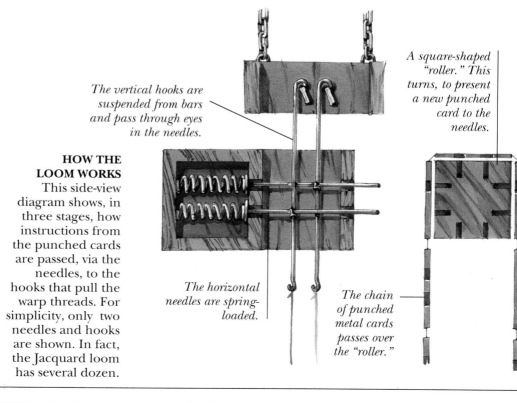

HOW THE LOOM WORKS
This side-view diagram shows, in three stages, how instructions from the punched cards are passed, via the needles, to the hooks that pull the warp threads. For simplicity, only two needles and hooks are shown. In fact, the Jacquard loom has several dozen.

The vertical hooks are suspended from bars and pass through eyes in the needles.

The horizontal needles are spring-loaded.

A square-shaped "roller." This turns, to present a new punched card to the needles.

The chain of punched metal cards passes over the "roller."

BLAISE PASCAL
(1623-1662)
French scientist and philosopher Pascal was only nineteen when he built a mechanical calculating machine known as the "Pascalina." The machine was based more on the working of a mill than on sophisticated clockwork.

ADA LOVELACE
(1815-1852)
The daughter of the poet Byron was a keen mathematician and a friend of Charles Babbage. She described his "analytical machine:" it "weaves algebraic patterns just as the Jacquard loom weaves flowers and leaves."

CHARLES BABBAGE
(1792-1871)
An English mathematician, Babbage invested a fortune in his attempt to create his "analytical machine," able to carry out any sequence of arithmetical operations automatically.

CALCULATORS
The punched card principle was the basis of the first electromechanical computers, which were designed to carry out simple but long statistical computations. American Herman Hollerith invented a machine of this kind for calculating data from the U.S. census in 1890.

A MACHINE NEVER BUILT
Babbage's "analytical machine" was cleverly conceived, but it was never built because it was beyond the technology of the time. Entirely mechanical in design and requiring hundreds of gears, it would have been bulky, difficult to operate, heavy, and extremely fragile.

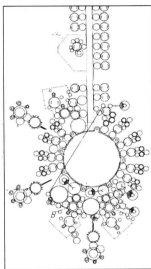

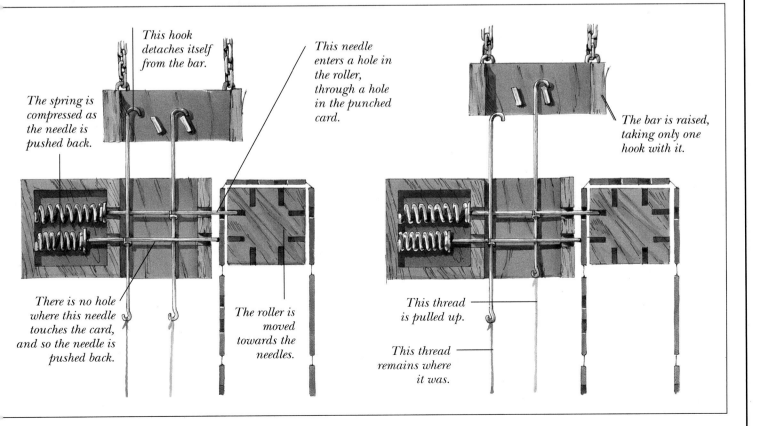

This hook detaches itself from the bar.

This needle enters a hole in the roller, through a hole in the punched card.

The spring is compressed as the needle is pushed back.

The bar is raised, taking only one hook with it.

There is no hole where this needle touches the card, and so the needle is pushed back.

The roller is moved towards the needles.

This thread is pulled up.

This thread remains where it was.

ROBOTS: IMAGINED AND REAL

For well over a hundred years, developments in science and technology have inspired poets and other writers to imagine what the world might be like in the future. Some are enthusiastic about what might happen. Others foresee catastrophe. In 1920, the word "robot" was coined by Karel Čapek for an efficient, artificial being, obedient to the will of its constructor. Since then, robots have captured the popular imagination. In science fiction novels and films they are presented as intelligent automata with exceptional abilities. Some turn against their creator. The word "robot" is also used by scientists and engineers involved in factory automation, but for them it has a more precise and limited meaning. It is a machine tool. It is powerful, works on its own, and can be made to perform many different tasks, but it definitely has no intelligence.

STAR WARS
C3PO and R2-D2 are the most famous robots in the history of the movies. They appeared in *Star Wars*, one of the most popular films of all time, made in 1977 by director George Lucas.

METROPOLIS
Metropolis was the masterpiece of the U.S. film director (born in Vienna) Fritz Lang. First shown in 1926, it features a magnificent automaton in human form, which became the prototype of future movie robots.

FRANKENSTEIN
In the early nineteenth century, scientists still tended to compare the human body to a machine. Mary Shelley took her cue from this idea for her novel *Frankenstein, or the Modern Prometheus* (1817). Doctor Frankenstein brings to life a being which he has built from parts of corpses. Although the experiment is technically a success, the creature brings distress and ruin, finally rebelling against its creator.
In a film of the novel, Boris Karloff played the monster (above), 1931.

Susan Calvin interviewing a robot; an illustration for one of Isaac Asimov's stories, 1947.

CHESS
In 1912, the Spanish engineer Leonardo Torres Quevedo built an automaton capable of playing a game of chess with a reduced number of pieces: a castle and a king for the robot, and a king for its human opponent. This was the first of a new breed of automaton, no longer made to mimic human movements and appearance but designed to process information and perform intellectual exercises.

ISAAC ASIMOV
(1920-1992)
One of the best-known writers of science fiction stories is Isaac Asimov. He created the character of Susan Calvin, a scientist who builds robots. Asimov noticed the predictability of stories about robots, which always rebelled against their creator, and so, in 1940, he formulated the three laws of robotics:
1) a robot cannot harm a human being, nor can it allow harm to be done to a human being through its negligence;
2) it must obey the orders of a human being, except when such orders contradict the first law;
3) it must defend its own existence, unless such defence contradicts the first or second laws.

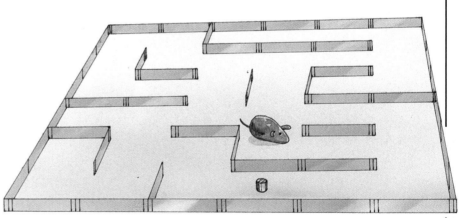

AN ARTIFICIAL MOUSE
One of the first attempts to build a machine capable of imitating the behavior of a living creature was made by Thomas Ross. His idea was inspired by the maze test, which psychologists used to study the learning capacity of rats. In 1938 he created an electromechanical mouse, which found its way to a particular point of the maze by a process of trial and error.

REMOTE MANIPULATION

Scientists investigating radioactivity at the beginning of the twentieth century did not know about the dangers of radiation. They handled radioactive materials, unaware of the deadly risk they were taking. Then the dangers became known and, as nuclear research developed in the 1940s, scientists needed a means of handling radioactive materials while they sheltered behind thick glass and lead screens. This led to the invention of mechanical remote manipulators: artificial arms fitted with pincers, which could be operated from a distance. From then on, tremendous progress was made in remote manipulation. Electric and electronic control systems increased the distance there could be between the operator and the artificial arm, so that it even became possible from Earth to control the arms of probes on the Moon. More recently, human-operated remote manipulators have been replaced by computer-operated ones – machines programed to perform certain tasks on their own.

THE BEGINNING
Designed for handling substances from a distance, the first remote manipulators were mechanical pincers controlled directly by a human operator. The maximum possible distance between the operator and the pincers was about ten feet.

MARIE CURIE
(1867-1934)
With her husband Pierre (1859-1906), Marie Curie studied the radiation emitted by uranium and discovered the radioactive elements polonium and radium. For this, they won the Nobel Prize for Physics in 1903. Marie was awarded a second Nobel Prize in 1911 for her work on radium. She died of leukemia, almost certainly caused by exposure to radiation.

EXOSKELETON
The arm of a remote manipulator moves in response to the movement of the operator. In a similar way, this exoskeleton (meaning an external skeleton) copies and magnifies its wearer's movements, enabling him or her to lift great weights.

AN ARM'S LENGTH
The longer a mechanical arm is, the more difficult it is to control accurately. You can appreciate this, if you have ever tried to pick fruit using a long pole.

TELEOPERATORS
Manipulators where a human operator controls the mechanical arm, not directly, but from a different location, are sometimes called "teleoperators." Lunokhod (above) was an example, its movements on the Moon were controlled from the Earth.

MASTER-SLAVE
The first mechanical manipulator was made by the Raymond Goertz group in 1947, not far from the first American nuclear reactor, which had been built by Enrico Fermi in Chicago in 1942.

It was known as master-slave. Ten years later, the first electrically controlled manipulator was built in the same laboratory. It was then possible to operate the mechanical pincers from a far greater distance.

THE CONTROL
The control handle for operating a remote manipulator is very similar to the joystick of video games – for example, a flight-simulator game. Of course, in the video game, the airplane does not really exist and the controls are simple. But it is not impossible that, at some future date, real planes might be controlled by real pilots working all the necessary controls from an armchair at home!

Mobile trolley.

Height controller.

Overhead gantry.

Elbow controller.

Pincers.

Thick glass screen.

Control handle worked by human operator.

KEEPING ARMS SHORTER
It is often better to avoid the use of over-long manipulator arms, which are difficult to move accurately. Instead, a shorter arm is fixed to a traveling gantry, which can take the arm close to the work site.

THE COMING OF COMPUTERS

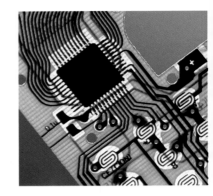

The first long-range nuclear missiles appeared during the period of the Cold War. They could travel at supersonic speeds, and this made American generals aware of the weakness of their defenses. Even if an incoming enemy missile was detected by American radar systems, there would not be time to react and intercept it, because of its great speed. The generals turned for help to scientists, who were then working on the first data processors. The experts set up a network of processors which were in communication both with the American radar systems and with U.S. fighter planes in the air. This automated the entire chain of decision-making. If a missile was launched against the U.S.A., the computers would be informed of the fact by radar; they would then automatically order the nearest aircraft to intercept the missile. The whole system reacted exactly like a human being, but much more quickly. This was the first intelligent automated system, a rival perhaps to the robots of science fiction.

THE COLD WAR
From the end of the Second World War until the early 1980s, there was hostility between the U.S.A. and the U.S.S.R. This Cold War encouraged the development of ever more powerful weapons.

THE COMPUTER
A computer is an electronic machine which is able to memorize and process information at a far greater speed and in much greater quantities than the human brain.

INFORMATION TECHNOLOGY
The branch of science concerned with the processing and transmission of data (information) by electronic processors or computers is known in English as Information Technology. In French the term is "Informatique" – a word coined by Philippe Dreyfus in 1962. It is a combination of "information" and "automatic."

During the Second World War, the Allied powers used radar to detect attacking enemy aircraft. The information was relayed immediately to Strategic Command.

ENIAC
Electronic Numerical Integrator And Calculator was designed by U.S. scientists J.P.Eckert and J.W. Mauchly and built in 1946. The first data-processing machine based on electronic circuits rather than electro-mechanical systems, it could perform 5,000 calculations in one second! It was enormous and contained 18,000 vacuum tubes.

UNIVAC
The Universal Automatic Computer, 1951, was the first to be mass-produced and to store data on magnetic tape. It handled numerical and alphabetical information.

Pilots at the fighter base ran to board their aircraft. By the time they took off, several minutes had passed since the enemy plane had been detected. However, there was still time to intercept the enemy, as, in those days, aircraft flew only at about 400 mph. As missiles were developed, the response time was cut dramatically.

GENERATIONS OF COMPUTERS

Although the first computer was built only about fifty years ago, we often speak of computer "generations."

I
First generation computers, such as ENIAC, used vacuum tubes.

II
In the second generation, vacuum tubes were replaced by transistors.

III
The third generation was marked by the introduction of integrated circuits.

IV
The computers of today are based on micro-processors.

V
The generation of computers now under development will make use of superconductors.

From Strategic Command, the order to "scramble" was sent out to the fighter base.

FROM DEATH RAY TO RADAR

In 1935, the British government asked scientist Robert Watson-Watt if it were possible to produce a death ray capable of destroying enemy aircraft. Watson answered that this was not possible, but that he could create a system for giving advance warning of an enemy attack. In just a few months, the first radar transmitter was built. Three years later, the British coastline was covered with a network of radar stations. These proved to be of vital importance during the Second World War.

FIRST USES

The computing power of early data-processing systems was used mainly for forecasting hurricanes and for predicting paths of missiles. Little use was made of the systems' potential for decision-making and giving orders.

EXPLORING SPACE AND THE SEA BED

Much of the progress in robotic technology is the result of the tremendous research and development required for space programs. The exploration of space required more advanced remote controlled devices and more sophisticated programed machines. The first Moon probes, in the 1960s, were controlled directly from Earth, although this was somewhat difficult since the radio signals took about 30 seconds to arrive. Later, when scientists planned to use the Viking spacecraft to explore Mars, they calculated that it would take 30 minutes for a radio message from Earth to reach that planet! In that case, it would be impossible to use remote control to operate the Viking lander. Instead, the craft was programed to function like a robot and carry out a series of tasks without human control: taking photographs, collecting data about the atmosphere, taking soil samples and analyzing them in a mini-laboratory, and finally, transmitting all the information gathered back to Earth.

SURVEYOR III
In 1967, Americans sent the lander Surveyor III to the Moon. It had an articulated arm (controlled from Earth) designed for taking samples from the Moon's surface and measuring the force required to do so.

THE VIKING LANDER
The American Viking probe landed on Mars in 1976. It had a telescopic arm with a revolving part at the end for gathering soil samples. These were then analyzed in the spacecraft's own laboratory.

VHF antenna.

Television camera.

Landing gear.

Telescopic manipulator arm.

Pincer for gathering soil samples.

Landing engine.

LUNOKHOD
This Soviet lunar roving vehicle was landed on the Moon in 1970. It moved around slowly in response to orders received from Earth with many seconds' delay. For "eyes," Lunokhod had two television cameras. A bank of photoelectric cells generated the energy needed to power the vehicle.

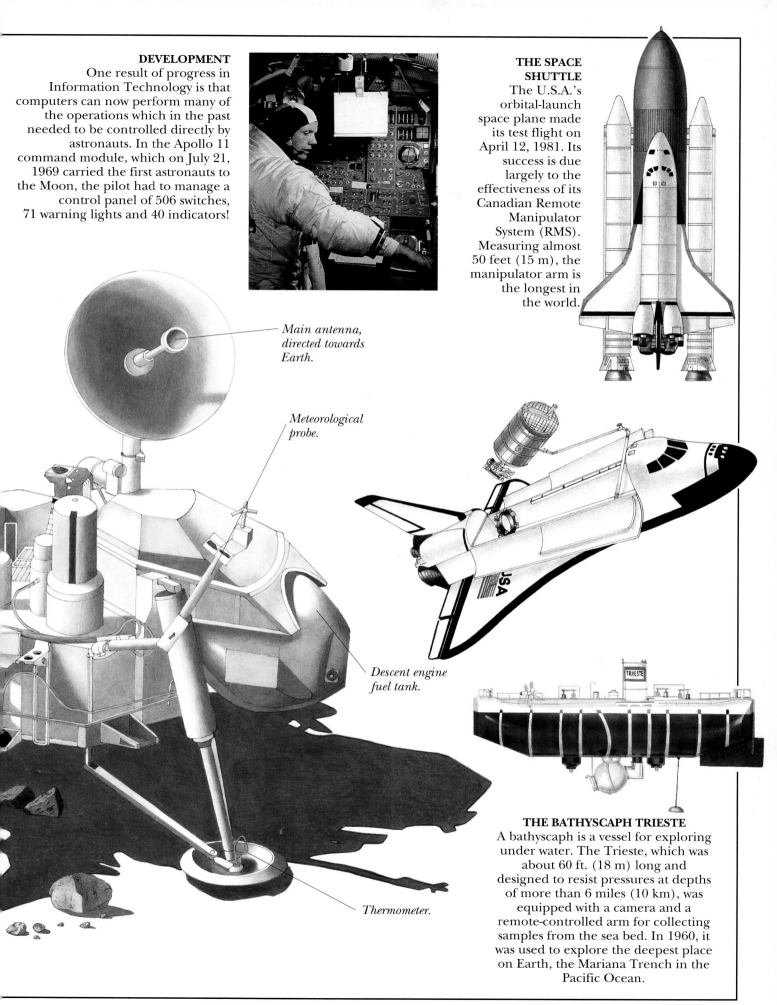

DEVELOPMENT

One result of progress in Information Technology is that computers can now perform many of the operations which in the past needed to be controlled directly by astronauts. In the Apollo 11 command module, which on July 21, 1969 carried the first astronauts to the Moon, the pilot had to manage a control panel of 506 switches, 71 warning lights and 40 indicators!

THE SPACE SHUTTLE

The U.S.A.'s orbital-launch space plane made its test flight on April 12, 1981. Its success is due largely to the effectiveness of its Canadian Remote Manipulator System (RMS). Measuring almost 50 feet (15 m), the manipulator arm is the longest in the world.

Main antenna, directed towards Earth.

Meteorological probe.

Descent engine fuel tank.

Thermometer.

THE BATHYSCAPH TRIESTE

A bathyscaph is a vessel for exploring under water. The Trieste, which was about 60 ft. (18 m) long and designed to resist pressures at depths of more than 6 miles (10 km), was equipped with a camera and a remote-controlled arm for collecting samples from the sea bed. In 1960, it was used to explore the deepest place on Earth, the Mariana Trench in the Pacific Ocean.

ROBOTS IN MEDICINE

In operations today, surgeons try to cut open the patient as little as possible and so they must use fine instruments with great skill and precision. In operations on the eye or brain, it is often necessary to make tiny punctures in such a restricted space that the needle has to perform microscopic movements. In such operations, the surgeon cannot see directly what is happening, but looks at a picture transmitted via optic fibers. Miniature forceps are worked by remote control: they reproduce the movements of the larger forceps held by the surgeon. Another area of medicine where robotics has proved its worth is the design and fitting of prostheses. Artificial arms and legs can now be connected directly to existing nerve endings and muscles, and the brain can control them just as it would a natural limb.

REPLACING LOST LIMBS
Sometimes pirates of old are depicted with wooden legs and iron hooks for hands. Such rough-and-ready methods of replacing lost limbs were often used in the past.

VIRTUAL REALITY
By putting on special gloves and glasses that are really television screens, you can enter a world that does not exist, the world of virtual reality.

Television screen.

The surgeon wears sensitive gloves which send instructions from his hands to the manipulator in the operating theater.

ROBOTICS
Robotics is one branch of Information Technology. It is concerned chiefly with finding ways of increasing the ability of machines, or machine parts, to work on their own. In other words, robotics has to do with designing and making more intelligent machines.

A virtual image appears on the television screen. It is called "virtual" because it combines the television picture with an X-ray picture.

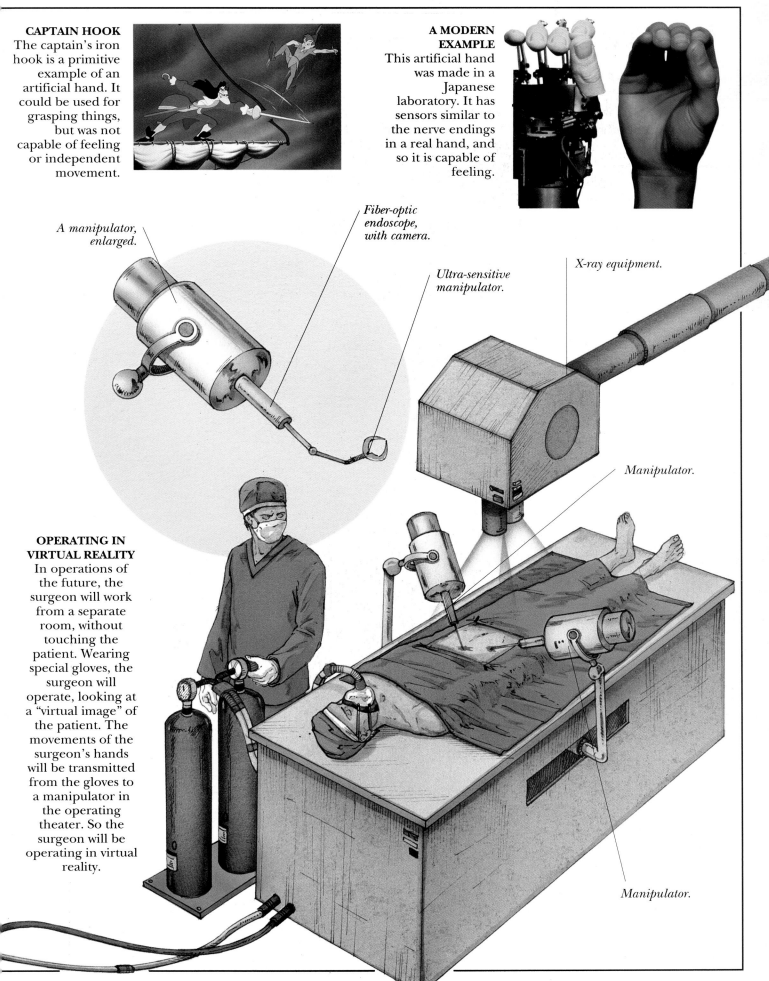

CAPTAIN HOOK
The captain's iron hook is a primitive example of an artificial hand. It could be used for grasping things, but was not capable of feeling or independent movement.

A MODERN EXAMPLE
This artificial hand was made in a Japanese laboratory. It has sensors similar to the nerve endings in a real hand, and so it is capable of feeling.

A manipulator, enlarged.

Fiber-optic endoscope, with camera.

Ultra-sensitive manipulator.

X-ray equipment.

Manipulator.

OPERATING IN VIRTUAL REALITY
In operations of the future, the surgeon will work from a separate room, without touching the patient. Wearing special gloves, the surgeon will operate, looking at a "virtual image" of the patient. The movements of the surgeon's hands will be transmitted from the gloves to a manipulator in the operating theater. So the surgeon will be operating in virtual reality.

Manipulator.

INDUSTRIAL ROBOTS

Robots are more and more commonly used in industry. Particularly in car manufacturing plants, automatic machines have almost completely replaced manual workers on assembly lines. Cars pass down the line one by one, and the waiting robots perform complex tasks according to the information which is stored in the memories of the computers controlling them. The robots bolt on parts, weld, paint, install seats and fix doors. To make them change from performing one task to another, all that is necessary is to switch a computer program and fix on a different terminal attachment (hand). Industrial robots of this kind are therefore extremely versatile, but they cannot yet be said to display much initiative. For them to function properly, the various components must be delivered to exactly the right spot on the assembly line.

AUTOMATION
The word "automation" was first used in the U.S.A. in 1947, for the process by which machines were taking over manual tasks. With the development of electronics and computer science, automation has come to mean more. Machines now can perform more than manual tasks. They also have control and adjustment functions.

MEMORIZING MOVEMENTS
Early robots had to be taught to perform a particular task. A technician moved the manipulator arm as necessary for the task, or used a teaching unit (above), and the robot's computer memorized the movements. Once memorized, the program could be repeated at will.

Hydraulic motor.

The elbow bends.

Electric motor.

Control console housing mini-computer.

The whole arm rotates.

The wrist moves in three directions.

UNIMATE
George C. Devol designed this first industrial robot. It was introduced in the U.S.A. in 1961, for unloading parts from a die-casting operation. A technician guided the gripper to the positions in which it was to operate and this stored the movements in Unimate's electronic memory. After this, Unimate could repeat the operation on its own.

CINCINNATI MILACRON
1974 saw the introduction of the Cincinnati Milacron: the first industrial robot controlled entirely by a mini-computer.

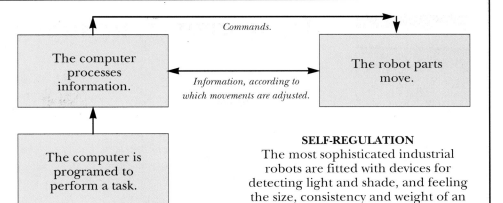

The computer processes information.

Commands.

The robot parts move.

Information, according to which movements are adjusted.

The computer is programed to perform a task.

CALCULATING MOVEMENTS

More advanced robots do not need to be given movements to memorize. A computer model of the component to be assembled is generated. From this, the robot can calculate the movements it needs to make to perform the prescribed task.

SELF-REGULATION

The most sophisticated industrial robots are fitted with devices for detecting light and shade, and feeling the size, consistency and weight of an object. Known as sensors, these devices enable the robot to receive messages from its immediate environment and adjust its behavior accordingly.

Motor.

Motor.

Memory control.

Manual controls.

Stop   Pause   Go

Mem. I

A

On·Off   Mem. II   Program

B

Technic Control Center

Automatic operation control.

TOY ROBOTS

Programable toys can be taught to perform movements and tasks, just like industrial robots. First the motorized robot toy must be put through a sequence of movements. Its computer memorizes them. The toy will then repeat the movements automatically.

PARALLEL ROBOTS

Robots in science fiction films may be super-intelligent, but they are always rather jerky in the way they move. In real life, too, robots' movement needs improving. A disadvantage of the manipulator arms of industrial robots is that they cannot perform continuous, flowing actions like those of a human arm. To overcome this problem and achieve greater precision in movement, scientists have developed robots with a different structure. The moving parts or joints of a manipulator robot are linked in line, with the hand at the end of the line. Instead of this arrangement, the new type of robot – called a "parallel robot" – has moving parts which are each joined directly to the final part of the system. Rather like the strings of a puppet, the robot parts work side by side to produce flowing movement. Parallel robots have been used to create high-precision "wrist joints," flight simulators and also some special "virtual reality" displays.

The computer lets the instructor know how the pilot is reacting to the simulated in-flight situations.

FLOWING MOVEMENT

By controlling four strings simultaneously, a skilled puppeteer can make a puppet perform flowing movements. The parts of a parallel robot work together in a similar way to the strings.

The instructor orders the computer to simulate specific flight conditions, for instance, those associated with night flying.

A STEWART PLATFORM

The structure of a parallel robot can be seen in the "Stewart platform." This consists of six variable-length, computer-controlled legs, which support the platform that is the final part of the system. A Stewart platform is sometimes used as a supporting "left hand" in high-precision assembly work.

FLIGHT SIMULATORS

Used for training pilots, flight simulators consist of a cockpit fixed to a Stewart platform. They simulate the take-off, in-flight behavior and landing of a real aircraft. Lifelike effects are achieved with the help of the parallel robot.

A TOY LIKENESS

This simple toy gives an idea of how a parallel robot like the Stewart platform moves. The toy's base conceals a spring. Compressing it from underneath changes the way the toy animal stands.

Images simulating in-flight conditions are created by the computer and projected onto a curved screen.

Looking through the cockpit window, the pilot sees the virtual images projected on the screen.

RIDE THAT MOVIE

Parallel robots are also used for entertainment. There are currently four theaters (in Tokyo, Toronto, Paris and at Disneyland) where spectators have to fasten their seat belts before the show begins! Thanks to a parallel robot, the whole theater moves in response to the material shown on screen, exactly simulating the motion, for example, of an airplane, a cart traveling through the mountains of Russia, or a formula-one racing car.

AIR FORCE

Controlled by the computer, the telescopic legs of the parallel robot carry out the instructor's orders and react to the pilot's maneuvers.

AIMING ANTENNAS

Parabolic antennas need to be precisely aimed at their targets, usually a satellite. Parallel robots can make the necessary continual fine adjustments to the antenna's supports.

ROBOTS ON THE MOVE

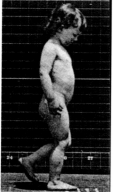

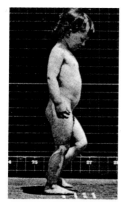

The day of robots which walk on two legs like human beings is still a long way off. Such robots would need computer systems of extraordinary complexity, capable of sending a constant stream of hundreds of instructions to each mechanical muscle involved in movement. The major problem would be maintaining the robot's balance. For the time being, the simplest way to make a robot mobile is to fit it with wheels, whose speed and direction can easily be controlled by a computer. Even so, wheels are not suited to all environments. The small, light Sojouner ìroverî that explored Mars in July of 1997 traveled on six independently controlled and suspended wheels, but this limited its ability to climb over obstacles higher than its wheels. Future robots are planned that will carry more weight and travel on tracks over rougher terrain, they may look like small tanks.

HEXAPOD
In the 1980s, robots with six legs, like insects, were built in American and Russian laboratories. This design solved the problem of how to maintain the robot's balance when it moved. It is much easier to move one leg if you have five others to rest on!

MOVING ON TWO LEGS
The ability to stand on two legs and move around in this upright position is a great asset for human beings, as it frees our hands for other tasks. However, walking on two legs is not nearly so safe or simple as moving around on four. Our two-legged gait requires that our brain must be constantly engaged in maintaining balance.

THE FIRST TWO-LEGGED ROBOT
Robot WL-5 (above) was built in 1971 by scientists at the Kato laboratory in Japan. This was the first computer-controlled robot that could walk on two legs—at a rate of one 6.5 inch (17 cm) step every 40 seconds!— Twelve years later, the same laboratory came up with WL-10, a robot which could take a 19.5 inch (50 cm) step every 4 seconds.

JKL
JKL is a mobile robot designed for the future exploration of Mars. It will be able to get around natural obstacles on its own.

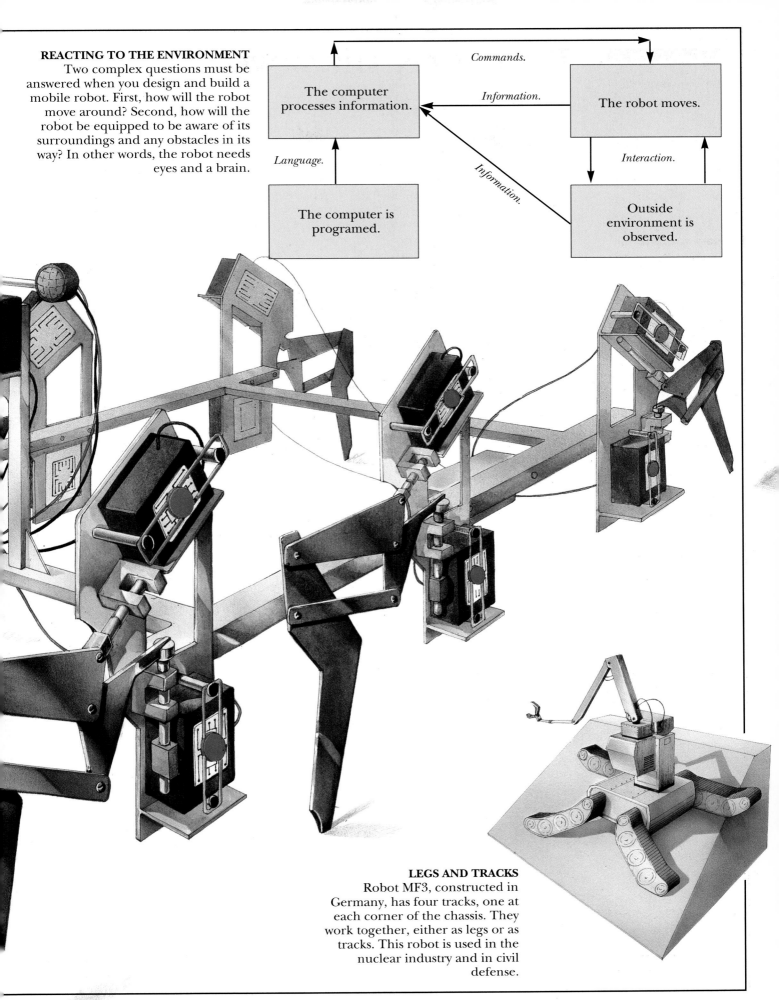

REACTING TO THE ENVIRONMENT

Two complex questions must be answered when you design and build a mobile robot. First, how will the robot move around? Second, how will the robot be equipped to be aware of its surroundings and any obstacles in its way? In other words, the robot needs eyes and a brain.

Commands.

Information.

The computer processes information.

The robot moves.

Language.

Information.

Interaction.

The computer is programed.

Outside environment is observed.

LEGS AND TRACKS

Robot MF3, constructed in Germany, has four tracks, one at each corner of the chassis. They work together, either as legs or as tracks. This robot is used in the nuclear industry and in civil defense.

A ROBOT THAT IS ALMOST HUMAN

1780
The harpsichord player created by Henri-Louis Droz was one of the most complex and perfect automata ever made. It represented the highest achievement of the precision engineering which developed from clockmaking. The automaton had a mechanical memory, in the form of a cylinder, but it could not act with any initiative.

On March 16, 1985, almost two hundred years after Droz built his harpsichord player, a concert was given to open the International Exhibition of Science and Technology at Tsukuba in Japan. The pianist – Wasubot – was a robot! So, what progress had been made in the manufacture of artificial beings, from the eighteenth-century automaton to the late twentieth-century robot? Without doubt, Wasubot was less attractive than the graceful doll created by Droz. But what a difference there was in the way they performed! The harpsichord player could play only the few tunes permitted by its mechanical programs; Wasubot could read and interpret any musical score, and even keep time with other musicians. Wasubot really does have certain human characteristics: he can see and read (although only musical scores) and has some initiative. He regulates himself to stay in time with the orchestra, reacting correctly to unexpected changes of rhythm.

1985
Wasubot was the result of research begun by scientists at the Kato laboratories in Japan in the 1960s. In building the robot, they used knowledge they had gathered on artificial hands, mobility and computer science.

The musical score.

WASUBOT'S EYE
A TV-camera "eye" generates a digital image of each note, made up of black or white dots (pixels). The image is sent to the computer, which processes the data and instructs Wasubot's mechanical "muscles" to play the right note.

The eye of the electronic television camera trained on the score.

The camera translates the real image of the score into a digital image.

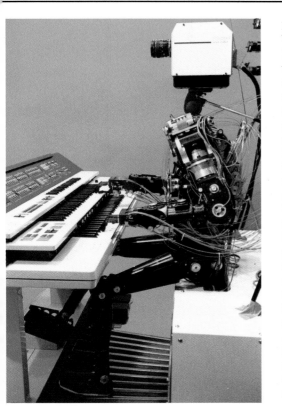

IN TIME
Wasubot's "brain" is a computer which processes enormous amounts of data at great speed. It is programed to extract information from the digital images of the music that it receives from the TV camera. This is then processed by another program which controls Wasubot's mechanical apparatus, making it play the right notes on the piano. All this happens so fast that Wasubot keeps in perfect time with the rest of the orchestra.

THE CONCERT
On the large television screen Wasubot's hands could be seen playing J.S.Bach's Air in B minor. He was accompanied by the symphony orchestra of the Japanese broadcasting company NHK.

The computer receives the digitalized data, and processes it to work out the form of each note.

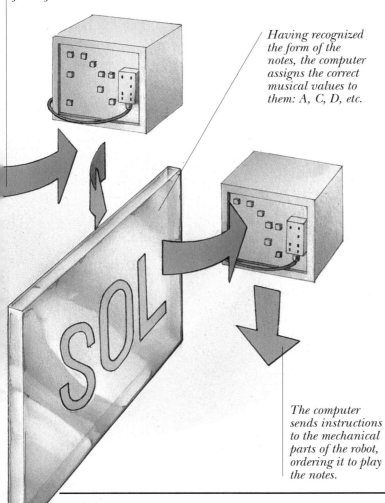

Having recognized the form of the notes, the computer assigns the correct musical values to them: A, C, D, etc.

The computer sends instructions to the mechanical parts of the robot, ordering it to play the notes.

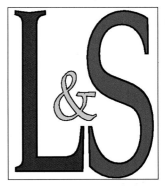

SEEING
Seeing means recognizing images received from outside. The process requires an eye to capture the images (in the case of Wasubot, a television camera) and a brain which is able to recognize them (a computer). Present-day computers are capable of recognizing simple images, for instance, a musical score.

READING
Seeing a musical score implies simply recognizing it as a sheet of paper on which various symbols have been printed. Reading the score means being able to interpret the symbols. Wasubot's brain is able to read the score because he has been taught musical notation and the musical "alphabet" is relatively simple.

WHO'S IN THE DRIVER'S SEAT?

People who are used to driving a car may often forget how complex a task this is. In contrast, engineers whose job is to design car-driving robots are very aware of the complexity. The main difficulty for these engineers lies in teaching the robots to recognize the external environment so that they can make decisions automatically: turning in response to a bend in the road, keeping a safe distance behind the car ahead, braking when animals or pedestrians step out into the road, and so on. Building a robot with these abilities is theoretically possible, but would need computers of exceptional power. Car manufacturers are therefore going for something simpler: designing a robot which behaves more like an assistant driver. It could be called a "guardian angel." This type of robot intervenes only in emergencies: for example, when the human driver is distracted, is in danger of nodding off, or, for whatever reason, drives without enough care and attention.

DIFFICULTIES
The difficulty when creating a robot driver is to teach it to detect and react to signals from the external environment: the shape of the road, road signs, hazards, pedestrians and so on. Computers that would enable the robot to see, recognize and process such a vast amount of information, and react in real time, would have to be extremely large and powerful – so large, in fact, that a truck would be needed to transport them.

THE DRIVER-LESS CAR
Owning a car-driver robot would be like having your own chauffeur: a luxury, but not one that is to everyone's taste. In fact, car manufacturers believe that the majority of drivers, including those who could afford to employ a chauffeur, actually prefer to drive themselves.

CARMINAT
Some French cars are already fitted with the Carminat system. It consists of a screen showing the main road network in the Paris area. The roads are displayed in different colors according to road traffic conditions at the time. Roads are shown in green, if traffic on them is flowing freely. Orange denotes that conditions are less favorable. Red signifies traffic jams, and black means that a street is completely closed to traffic.

Laser system measuring the distance from the car in front. It might be programed to keep a distance of 40 yards at a speed of 70 mph. If the car gets too close, the brakes are automatically applied.

Television camera monitoring the right-hand side of the car.

The monitor screen displays information about general traffic conditions on the road and how they affect the car.

Television camera keeping an eye on the white line. If the driver inadvertently crosses the line when another car is coming up behind, the robot automatically steers the car back into its own lane.

Television camera to monitor the car as it passes. Information is fed to the on-board computer, which advises the driver to take care or actually intervenes to prevent him or her making an error.

AA11E41

ARTIFICIAL INTELLIGENCE

It was in 1956 that the term "artificial intelligence" was first used. It described a field of scientific research with an extremely ambitious aim: to discover how the human mind works and make an artificial replica of it. The difficulties of this project – which involved psychology, linguistics, logic and computer science – proved so great that scientists were forced to scale down their objectives. Nowadays, artificial intelligence is no longer concerned with making a copy of the human mind. Instead, the aim is to build computer systems which will produce reactions similar to those one might expect from a human being. Although these systems might seem to have human-like intelligence, the reactions they make are in fact produced by mechanisms which are completely different from human reasoning and which are based entirely on Information Technology.

BIRTH OF AN IDEA

At a conference held at Dartmouth, N.H., in 1956, scientists John McCarthy and Marvin Minsky launched the idea of designing artificial intelligence. They believed that every single characteristic of the human mind could be precisely identified and therefore simulated by machines.

WHAT MAKES A MACHINE INTELLIGENT?

To be "intelligent," a machine must be able to cope with unexpected situations. For example, two components on an assembly line might arrive in a position different from normal. An intelligent machine would recognize that these were the normal two parts, and not a different-shaped one.

THE PILOT

A pilot can tell whether an aircraft is friend or foe by its appearance and the markings on its wings and fuselage. The human brain recognizes such features easily. However, if an aircraft has no markings and its shape is not familiar, the pilot cannot identify it.

EXPERT SYSTEMS

One of the most interesting applications of artificial intelligence is in creating expert systems. All the knowledge of an expert in a certain field is fed into a computer, which can then be asked to solve problems in the same way you would consult an expert.

DIAGNOSIS

Expert systems have been developed in the area of medicine, to make diagnoses and prescribe treatments. The patient states the symptoms he or she is experiencing and this information is fed into a computer. The computer consults its store of knowledge, diagnoses the illness and prescribes a remedy.

THE TURING TEST

In 1950 the British mathematician Alan Turing (1912-1954) proposed this test. A human being typed questions into a teletype machine. Another human being and a computer, both behind a screen, sent back their answers. If the questioner could not tell which were the human answers, then the machine could be called "intelligent."

A MISSILE

A missile has a sensor which detects and "locks on" to the heat coming from an aircraft's engine. This is how it targets an aircraft. However, as a missile cannot recognize shapes, there is a danger that it could find and destroy an aircraft belonging to its own side.

THE ROBOTS OF TOMORROW

Robots of the kind you see in science fiction, with their amazing intelligence, are not just around the corner. In reality, there is a long way to go before there are machines that will be able to understand and react to their environment, making appropriate decisions. Robots in the future will certainly be more complex than any machine yet built, and more and more compact and independent. It is likely that they will come to perform most of the simple, repetitive, boring and dangerous tasks that are currently undertaken by human beings.

GLOSSARY

ALCHEMY The word is of Arabic origin. It describes attempts to change common metals into gold. More magical than scientific, alchemy was the medieval forerunner of modern chemistry.

AUTOMATION The use of mechanical, electrical or electronic equipment to reduce human involvement in a manufacturing process.

AUTOMATON A machine, with a hidden mechanism, that imitates the movements of human beings or animals. The plural can be either "automata" or "automatons."

AUTONOMOUS A machine is said to be autonomous when it can operate without constant fresh inputs of energy, or when it can perform a program of work unsupervised.

CAM An irregularly shaped part attached to a rotating shaft. The shape of the cam allows it to contact another part of the machine once in every rotation, converting the rotary movement into a repeating force at a single point.

CODE An agreed system of signs or symbols for representing information transmitted from a sender to a receiver.

COMPUTER Since 1968, this word has been used to describe machines with electronic systems for making calculations and processing data. (Before, they were called "calculators.")

CRANK A machine part on a rotating shaft, linked to another part of the machinery by a connecting rod. The crank and connecting rod serve to convert the rotary motion of the shaft into back-and-forward or up-and-down movement – for instance, of a piston.

DIGITAL In electronics, a digital device is one in which data are represented in the form of discrete (i.e. separate) signals. This makes the signals easier to transmit and process.

ELECTRICITY First used by the English physicist William Gilbert (1544-1603), this word comes from the Greek *elektron*, meaning amber – a material which, when rubbed, attracts small pieces of paper. In general, it is a form of energy consisting of tiny particles, called electrons, that carry the energy in what we call an electric "charge."

ELECTRONICS The science concerned with the study of electrons (minute particles charged with electricity) and their behavior with practical applications. It is to electronics that we owe the major technological developments of the twentieth century: radio, television, stereophonic systems, computers, the telephone, automation and robotics.

ENDOSCOPE An instrument used to see inside a body cavity or hollow organ, for example, the sinuses.

FEEDBACK The process whereby a machine or system regulates itself by taking into account the results of its past behavior.

INFORMATION TECHNOLOGY Often abbreviated to IT. This is an area of science concerned with the processing and automatic transmission of data by electronic computer systems.

INTEGRATED CIRCUIT A complete system of interconnected electronic elements designed to perform a particular function.

MACHINE Any device of a certain complexity designed to carry out specific tasks and improve on normal human performance in terms of speed, precision or strength. The ancient Greeks distinguished between simple machines (the lever, pulley or inclined plane) and more complex ones combining a number of simpler devices (for example, the hoist or crane).

MECHANICAL ENGINEERING The branch of engineering concerned with the construction of machines and mechanisms.

MECHANISM A group of moving parts that work together to perform a function in a machine.

MICROPROCESSOR The central processing unit of a computer, manufactured on a single integrated circuit chip (or several chips).

MILL A machine used for grinding grain and other crushable materials. Mills may be hand-operated or powered by wind or water.

OPTICAL FIBERS Long, thin threads of glass used to transmit light waves.

PHOTOELECTRIC CELL A device which transforms light energy into an electrical current. The voltage depends on the intensity of the light.

PROGRAM An analytical description of the way in which an activity is performed. In the case of a machine, the term refers to the set of precise instructions which enable it to carry out a given task.

PROSTHESIS This word originally meant the addition of a sound or syllable at the beginning of a word, for example, to make it easier to pronounce. Since the eighteenth century the word has also been used to describe the replacement of a missing organ, or part of an organ, with an artificial substitute – and to describe the artificial organ itself.

PUNCHED CARDS Cards with holes in them, which were the first method devised for communicating binary – yes or no – information to machines.

RADAR Apparatus used in ships and aircraft for detecting and identifying obstacles, even in darkness or fog. The equipment sends out radio waves and registers those that are reflected back from solid objects. The word is formed from the initial letters of RAdio Detecting And Ranging.

SELF-REGULATION The ability of a machine to adjust its behavior automatically in response to changes in the external environment, as a result of feedback.

SENSOR A device which registers variations in physical quantities (heat, pressure, etc.) and transmits the information to a measuring and control system.

SUPERCONDUCTOR The term used for metals or alloys which offer practically no resistance to electricity at very low temperatures.

TRANSISTOR A device consisting of a block of semiconducting material which boosts or changes electric currents and voltages. Transistors replaced vacuum tubes in the second generation of computers.

VACUUM TUBE Used in early computers and other electronic devices to boost or direct electrical current, they served much the same function as transistors later did. They were usually made of glass and generated heat, making them difficult to use in large numbers and in small spaces.

CREDITS

The original and previously unpublished illustrations in this book may be reproduced only with the prior permission of Donati Giudici Associati, who hold the copyright.

ILLUSTRATIONS: Boni-Galante Studio (Simone Boni 16tl; Lorenzo Cecchi-Ivan Stalio 4-5; Lorenzo Cecchi 10-11, 14-15, 26tl, 26tr, 26bl, 27tl, 27c, 44-45; Ivan Stalio 6-7, 8-9, 12-13, 24-25, 34bl); Francesca d'Ottavi 28-29, 32-33, 42-43; Carlo Ferrantini 20tr; Gianni Mazzoleni 8tr, 31br; Claudia Saraceni 16-17, 18-19, 20tl, 20bc, 21, 22cl, 22-23, 38-39, 40-41; Sergio 22tr; Daniela Sarcina 20cl, 22tl, 23cr, 26br, 30-31, 36-37; Donato Spedaliere 34tr, 38br, 42tl.

COVER: Claudi Saraceni.

TITLE PAGE: Ivan Stalio.

PHOTOGRAPHS: A.G.E./Granata Stock Photo 28tr; Alinari Archive 4cl; Ciro Antinozzi/ Grazia Neri; courtesy of Shigeki Sugano Lab, Waseda University, Tokyo 33tr, 38c, 40tr, 41tl, 41tr; D.R. 24tl; © Carlo Cantini 5c, 17br, 18c, 35c, 36tr, 37tl; Chapman Collection/Snap Photo/Grazia Neri 24c; DoGi Archive 5cr, 16tr, 16br, 18tl, 18tr, 19tl, 19br, 23tl, 23tc, 23tr, 23cl, 32tl, 32bl, 34tl, 35tl, 40tl; FRG/Grazia Neri 11tr; Granata Stock Photo 5tc, 15tr; © Luder 5cl, 18cl, 18bl, 19tr; © Peter Menzel/Grazia Neri 32tr; Muybridge 38tl, 38c, 38bl; NASA/GLMR/Grazia Neri 31tc; National Library of Medicine/Science Photo Library/Grazia Neri 26cl; © Chuck O'Rear/West Light/Granata Stock Photo 7tl; Photo INRIA 36cl, 36c, 36bl, 36bc; Photri/ Grazia Neri 29cr; Scala Archive 4tl; SS Archives Shooting Star/Grazia Neri 24cl, 24bl; © Sunset Boulevard/Sygma/Grazia Neri 33tl; Sygma/Grazia Neri 28cl, 28bl, 28bc; © Kevin Vandivier/Viesti Associates/Granata Stock Photo 29bc; Roger Viollet 21tr.

DoGi s.r.l. have made every effort to contact copyright holders. If any omissions have been made, this will be corrected at reprint.

INDEX